T0116481

# PERFECT PEACE

## The Gospel of Love

## KID HAITI

BALBOA.PRESS
A DIVISION OF HAY HOUSE

Balboa Press books may be ordered through booksellers or by contacting:

Balboa Press
A Division of Hay House
1663 Liberty Drive
Bloomington, IN 47403
www.balboapress.com
844-682-1282

Print information available on the last page.

ISBN: 979-8-7652-3336-8 (sc)
ISBN: 979-8-7652-3337-5 (hc)
ISBN: 979-8-7652-3335-1 (e)

Library of Congress Control Number: 2022915434

Balboa Press rev. date: 08/17/2022

TALK TO THE CITY, THE CITY AIN'T SILENT, THEY TALKING TO THEIR SHADOW, SLEEPWALKING IN THE BATTLE, SURRENDER TO THE MOST HIGH, CLOUDS OF LOVE, REMAIN SO FLY, SO MANY TALK ABOUT BEING REAL, FEEL LIKE THE WHOLE WORLD SIGNED THE DEAL, I GUESS I WASN'T INCLUDED, I GUESS YOU DID, DEVIL TRYING TO SWERVE IN MY LANE, SO MANY TEARS I THOUGHT IT WOULDN'T RAIN, FORGIVE ME GOD, TRYING TO DEAL WITH THE PAIN, IF CHRIST CAN DO IT, I CAN DO IT TOO, SEE IT IN THEIR EYES

THEY DON'T KNOW WHAT I'M BOUT TO DO, I TRY TO TELL THEM I LOVE YOU, WHEN I LOOK IN THEIR EYES, I DON'T EVEN KNOW YOU, BUT IT STILL REMAINS, I LOVE YOU.

SILENT TALK, CALL IT TRAIN OF THOUGHT, CHRIST PAINTED THE ART, THE CANVAS IS THE HEART, THEY WILL END WHEN THEY CAN'T START, DO YOU PLAY THE PART OR DO YOU SEE WITHIN THE DARK, THE SAME WARNING FOR THIS GENERATION, NOAH'S ARK, YOU CAN'T FLY WITH NO WINGS, I BREAK SATURN'S RINGS, WATCH HOW THE FLOWER SINGS, THE WORLD IS ENDING SOON, AND YOU WON'T BE ABLE TO LIVE ON THE MOON, CREATIVITY SPARKS A REVOLUTION OF PEACE, BUT THEY CAN'T DELIVER, THE WATER WITHIN, THEY SIT BY THE RIVER, GOD WILL ESTABLISH HIS THRONE ON

EARTH, NO ONE IS UNKNOWN UNTIL BIRTH, YOU CAN'T PLAY WITH THE HANDS OF WORDS, STILL SEE THE CLOUDS AND THE BIRDS, ASK GOD TO FORGIVE ME, LOOK IN MY HEART, THE HOLY SPIRIT WITH ME, AIN'T NOBODY MISS ME, THE LEGEND IS NO MYTH, HEAVEN'S ANGELS IS WHO I'M WITH.

I'M A THREAT TO THE SECRET SOCIETY, CHRIST IS THE TRUTH, HOW DARE THEY LIE TO ME, I GOT A LION ROARING INSIDE ME, THEY AIN'T GOT THE HEART TO SAY GOOD BYE TO ME, THAT'S WHY I GAVE THEM THE LOTTERY, I WIN YOU LOSE, Y'ALL BEEN SLEEPING ON ME, I'M THE SNOOZE, NO TRUTH IN THE NEWS, HOW MANY VIEWS, SO TELL ME WHO GOT THE REAL JUICE, WHY THEY AIN'T TELL ME YOU GOT TO SUFFER TO SING THE BLUES.

DON'T BOW DOWN TO ILLUMINATI, IT'S A NEW TOWN, I DON'T KNOW NOBODY, BUT I KNOW CHRIST EVEN IF I LOSE MY LIFE, ALOT OF PAIN, I CAN'T CONTAIN, ONE SOUL, TWO LANES, I'M HEADED FOR THE SKY, WATCH MY SPIRIT FLY, TEARS FROM THE RAIN WATCH MY HEART CRY, GOD WHY, I NEED THE ANSWER, THEY NEED THE CANCER, TRYING TO FIGURE OUT WHERE I'M STANDING, AIN'T NOTHING LEFT SO I'M LANDING, SEE ME LIKE A LION, I DON'T FEAR THEM, I'M SILENT, I DON'T HEAR THEM, SO WHEN THEY TALK I FEEL NO DIFFERENT, FOR ME I KNOW I WAS BORN GIFTED, RESURRECTION, THE LORD DID IT, I PRAY FOR THEM EVEN IF THEY AIN'T WITH IT, CAUSE I KNOW TIME IS UP, AND WHEN THE ANGELS CALL ME I'M COMING UP, DIRECT FLIGHT, BLESSED BEYOND THE CLOUDS.

WHERE WE WENT, DON'T ASK THE GOVERNMENT, THESE WOLVES SMELL THE SCENT, WE ROAR UNTILL MOUNTAINS COLLASPE, WHO WE ARE DON'T ASK, BUT NO SECRET LIKE ILLUMINATI, NO BODY, SPIRIT RUNNING THROUGH MY STRUCTURE, NOT BUILT FOR SCULPTURE, ARTISTICALLY PAINTED, WORDS THAT FAINTED, THEY WROTE HATE IN THEIR HEART, TRYING TO CLOSE THEIR EYES IN THE DARK, WITH CHRIST GOD WILL NOT BE APART, I WAS WITH YOU FROM THE START, THEY WERE HIDING IN THE DARK, LET THEM KNOW FEAR IS ONLY TO BE ASCRIBED TO ME THE LORD, PAIN IS AN AWARD ONLY PRESENTED TO THE MAN OF CHRIST, DIDN'T LOOK TILL I COULDN'T SEE, TILL I WOULDN'T BE, SURRENDER SHALL BE THE ONLY KEY THAT SHALL SET US FREE, LOVE IS NOT BLIND, IT IS

THE ONLY THING THAT CAN SEE AND THE ONLY THING THAT WILL BE.

WEAPON OF FEAR, LOOK IN THE MIRROR, DON'T INTERFERE, WITH THE LORD'S WORK, AND ME, I'M GOING TO CHURCH, AND I'M PRAISING, TELL EM WHERE IT HURTS, IN MY HEART, IT GREW DARK, THE LORD TORE IT APART, LIT WITH A CANDLE, GET IT ON YOUR CHANNEL, WE DON'T WATCH NO MORE, CAUSE THEY LIED TO THE POOR, WHO CREATED THE WAR, THE RICH, WHO THEY WORSHIP, MONEY WITH SOME LIPSTICK, TELL ME WHAT THAT DO, SMEAR THE BLOOD OF THE INNOCENT, CRIES OF A MOTHER, I'D DIE FOR MY BROTHER.

PERSONALITY, MUSIC, RELIGION, WHAT'S YOUR DECISION, I AIN'T SWITCHING. DON'T WATCH TELEVISON, I DON'T SUPPORT, THE LAW OF

COURT, BUT OF COURSE, THE LORD IS MY FORCE, CHRIST OPEN DOORS, GOD MADE YOU, THEY PAID YOU, ENSLAVED YOU, HE BROKE THE CHAINS, DECEIT, SLEEP, WEAK, LET US RISE, AGAINST THE POWERS WHO TOOK DOWN THE TOWERS, CURRRENCY IS CURRENTLY, A PLAGUE, DESTROYED IN RAGE, DON'T BE CAUGHT ON THE CLOCK, TIME OR JAIL, I WAS CHOSEN BY THE MAN ON THE THRONE, EVEN IF I STAND ALONE, TOUCH MY SOUL, MIND BLOWN.

DEMOCRACY IS AN HYPOCRISY, OBVIOUSLY MY HEART IS THE ODYSSEY, CHRIST IS A SIGHT TO SEE, THEY CAN'T SILENCE ME, NO EVOLUTION THEORY, THEY FEAR ME, HEAR THE LION, HEARTBEAT DYING, BUT THE LORD RAISED ME TO BELIEVE, HEAVENLY SAVED, MENTALLY ENSLAVED, HELP THE POOR, WINGS THAT SOAR,

WHY MORE JAILS THAN SCHOOLS, WHY WIN WHEN YOU LOSE, BY WHOSE RULES DO WE LISTEN, IN SOCIETY THE HEART IS MISSING, NOT ENOUGH PRAYING, TOO MUCH WISHING TO THE STARS.

TEARS IN THE NIGHTS DON'T COME OFTEN, THEY AINT' SEEN ME CRY, NO COFFIN, NO CASKET, WHO YOU REALLY ARE THEY DON'T WANT YOU TO ASK IT, WE PLAYING ONE ON ONE, AIN'T NO TIME TO PASS IT, LISTENING TO MY SOUL WITH HEADPHONES, EVEN THE HIEROGLYPHICS AIN'T SET IN STONE, LIKE CHRIST SAID, HE WITHOUT SIN CAST THE FIRST STONE, SILENCE IS MUSIC ALONE, ON MY KNEES LOOKING TO GOD ON THE THRONE, ALL THIS, I ALREADY SAW THIS, THEY WORSHIP THE SUN, NOW THEY STARLESS, IF YOU KNEW THE SON OF GOD, YOU WOULD BE

ON THE STAR LIST, YOU ARE AWAKENED, JUST
NEED TO START THINKING, CAUSE EVEN THE
OCEAN DROWNS WHEN THE SHIP IS SINKING,
UNLESS YOU BECOME LIKE THE WATER, PRAY
TO HEAVEN, ONE DAY I'LL SEE MY DAUGHTER.

# 3 / 12

MEMORIES SHATTERED, I DIDN'T THINK IT WOULD MATTER, ESCAPING DEATH IS A MATTER OF GRAVITY, SEEING GOD IS THE ONLY GUARANTEE, STILL LOOKING FOR GUIDANCE, STILL LOOKING FOR SIRENS, HOPING FOR A CHANGE OF THOUGHT, I LOVE YOU, THAT'S A CHANGE OF HEART, WHEN YOU FIND CHRIST THERE IS NO DARK, PICTURE ME IN HEAVEN, CALL THAT A WORK OF ART, MY MIND IS TELEVSION FROM WHAT I SEEN SO FAR, I CRIED

SO MANY TEARS CAUSE I WORKED SO HARD, HARDLY EVER NOTICED, WE DIDN'T LISTEN BUT THEY TOLD US.

THERE WILL BE A DAY IN YOUR LIFE WHEN YOU HAVE TO DIE, THERE WILL BE A TIME IN YOUR LIFE WHEN YOU HAVE TO CRY, I HOPE YOU KNOW WHY, THE MOMENT TO SAY GOOD BYE, TORN BETWEEN THE MIRROR OF PAIN AND THE REFLECTION OF LOVE, I PRAY THAT THE LORD SENDS THE DOVE, THAT WHICH IS OF, NO MAN CAN RELATE, NO MAN CAN BE LATE, MY WINGS FLY TO THE OCEAN, WAITING FOR HEAVEN TO OPEN, CHRIST IS THE TRUTH UNSPOKEN, DON'T LEAVE WITH YOUR HEART BROKEN.

THUNDERSTORMS IN THE LONG NIGHT, DON'T TAKE A WRONG RIGHT, LONG FLIGHT, TRYING TO GET MY MIND RIGHT, LOOKING AT THE SCENE,

SEEN IT WHEN I CRY, DON'T KNOW WHEN I'M A DIE, EVERYTHING AIN'T WHAT IT SEEM, REST IN PEACE, MASTERPIECE, SO SILENT, I'M THE LAST TO SPEAK, BUT I WALK UP ON THESE STREETS, PLEASE TAKE YOUR SEATS, CHRIST BECAME GOD, THAT'S WHAT HEAVEN NEEDS, CARRY THE WORLD ON MY SHOULDER, CALL IT HEAVY KNEES, THE HOLY SPIRIT DOESN'T LEAVE, SPRING, SUMMER, FALL, CAN'T WAIT FOR THE LEAVES.

TOO MUCH PAIN IN HER EYES, TOO MUCH RAIN IN THE SKY, IF I SHALL LOSE CONTROL, I'M A FLY, TOO LATE TO DIE, TOO LATE TO CRY, TO SAY GOOD BYE, THIS IS MY ANTHEM, AND MY ANGELS WINGS, I'M STILL LEARNING HOW TO LAND THEM, I ESCAPE THROUGH THE ILLUSION LIKE A PHANTOM, CLOUDS LOOKING FOR THE

AIR, AND NOBODY REALLY HAS TO CARE, JUST AS LONG YOU KNOW THEY'LL BE THE DAY WHEN NO ONE IS THERE, KEEP LOOKING AND YOU'LL SEE WHO'S THERE, I SEEN YOU BEFORE THEY TOLD ME, NOT EVEN HELL'S GATES CAN HOLD ME, MY ENERGY WILL NOT ALLOW ANY TO ENTER, ONLY GOD WHO ALLOWED CHRIST TO BE THE ENTRANCE, YOU HYPNOTIZED IN A TRANCE, THE DEVIL LOST HIS MIND WHEN HE SEEN MY PLANS, TOUCH THE WORLD WITH NO HANDS, ONE DAY WE'LL ALL HOLD HANDS.

I TRY TO STAY POSITIVE, BUT THEY WATCHING IT, NO TIME ON THE CLOCK, EVERY THOUGHT, I STAY SO PASSIONATE, AND THERE IS NO CATCHING IT, CATCHER IN THE RYE, CATCH YOU IN A LIE, I'M A FLY WHEN I DIE, NO TEAR WHEN I CRY, HOLD MY HEAD UP TO THE SKY, TAKE

THEM SHADES OFF, LET ME SEE YOUR EYES, I'M SO SORRY YOU BEEN BLINDED BY THEM LIES, DEAR MISS, YOU CAN'T EVEN SEE THE SUN RISE, FLOWER IN MY HAND WATCH THE GUN DIE, BLOOD OF A SAINT, I'M NOT WHO YOU THINK.

# 4 / 12

THANK GOD FOR THEM COLD NIGHTS, THANK GOD FOR THEM GOLD NIGHTS, WALKING IN THE DARK, TALKING IN MY HEART, MATRIX UNLOCKED. POVERTY IS PROBABLY A POLICY WHICH IS PART OF ME, PARDON ME, UNDERSTANDING GOD IS IN ME, ONLY ONE WAY OUT, SOMETHING I CAN'T DOUBT, ENTER THE DARK, I'M NOT WHAT YOU THOUGHT, WAITING FOR THE ARRIVAL, WAITING FOR THE REVIVAL, CHRIST TOLD ME THEY HATED ON HIM AND

LOOK WHAT HAPPENED, NO APPLUASE FOR THE FAKE, AIN'T NOBODY CLAPPING, AND WHEN IT'S ALL SAID AND DONE, I'LL BE THE LAST ONE LAUGHING.

I TOOK A TEST, TESTIMONY, I LOOK AT THE WORLD, ME ONLY, FORGIVE ME FOR MY SINS WHEN I'M WALKING THORUGH THE WIND, COLD WORLD, WHOLE WORLD, ONE NIGHT THE MEMORIES THAT WE MADE, ONE NIGHT THE MEMORIES JUST FADE, COULDN'T COUNT MY BLESSINGS, DON'T DOUBT MY PRESENCE, DIE TODAY TO SEE TOMMORROW, THE PAIN, TEARS AND SORROW, LET ME ALLOW MYSELF TO REALIZE MYSELF, I'M BYSELF, BUT THE LORD GOT ME BLESSED, CHRIST THE RESURRECTION, LIGHT, CAMERAS, ACTION, YOU LOOKING TO SIN, YOU NEED TO LOOK WITHIN.

OPEN THE DOOR, WALK THROUGH THE FLOOR, EXCUSE ME, THEM ANGELS GONNA SOAR, THE YOUTH OH SO POOR, UNTIL THERE AIN'T EVEN NO MORE, BUT YOU THE ONLY ONE TO IGNORE, THE CONSEQUENCES NOT REALZING THE ICONIC MESSAGE, OR REALIZING THE QUESTION, BOW DOWN TO NO MAN, NO CHANGE, NO HOPE MAN, LOOKING FOR HEAVEN, WITHIN IS CHRIST, THERE IS NO SUCH THING AS FREEDOM OF RIGHTS, YOU CAN'T LOSE, ONLY IF YOU CHOOSE.

I'M A QUARTERBACK WITH AN AUTOGRAPH, ALMOST CAUGHT A HEART ATTACK, I LOOK BACK, MAN IN THE MIRROR, HANDS IN THE RIVER, PLAN TO DELIVER, FOREVER, TRAIN OF THOUGHT, PAIN OF HEART, THAT'S WHAT I THOUGHT, SO PATIENT, BEEN WAITING, GLOW IN THE DARK, SNOW IN YOUR HEART, NO PRICE FOR

THE THOUGHT, JUST CHRIST FOR THE HEART, NO PRICE FOR MY HEART.

I REALIZE, FEAR LOVE, HEAR LIES, I CAN SEE YOUR EYES, ONE MOMENT EVERYONE DIES, THAT'S WHY WE LIVE FOR THE MOMENT, SHE BEAUTIFUL, DON'T IT, TELL ME IF YOU FELL IN LOVE, TELL ME IF YOU FEELING LOVE, LOCKED IN PRISON, FREE LOVE, PAY ATTENTION IF I DON'T MENTION GOD, THANK GOD, ALL I'M WAITING FOR IS TO SAY WHEN, PASSION OF THE CHRIST, DOVES GON LET US IN.

HIDDEN FEARS, WRITTEN TEARS, I KNOW WE AIN'T TALKED FOR SOME YEARS, INSPIRATION, DEMONSTRATION, WHAT CAN SAVE THE NATION, DEDICATION, YOU CAN QUOTE ME ON THE

# 5 / 12

STATEMENT, PRAY TO MY HEAVENLY FATHER, THEY STILL WAITING, PAIN IN MY HEART WHEN IT RAINS IN THE DARK, HANDS IN MY SCARF, PLEASE TURN IT OFF, BEEN ON TOO LONG, THEY ALWAYS GOT A QUESTION, THEY KNOW I DON'T TALK MUCH, I'VE BEEN THROUGH THE STEPS, SECRETS BEEN KEPT, HESITATE WHEN THEY BREATHE, CUT THE TAPE THIS IS FREE, IF I AIN'T MENTION GOD THAT WOULD BE LIKE NOT LOOKING AT THE SKY, DIDN'T REALIZE

WHO I WAS, FOREVER THE REALEST, I'M PEACE TO THESE DEALERS, I SPEAK TO GORILLAS, I DON'T NEED NO PASSPORT, SEE YOU LOOKING STRANGE WHAT YOU ASK FOR, CHRIST IS ALL I ASK FOR.

THE WORLD DON'T GET IT, I'M SO POETIC, ANY HEART CAN FEEL IT, I'M JUST A MEDIC, THEY SAY I'M SO PATHETIC, BUT THESE WORDS THEY CAN'T EVEN TOUCH OR EDIT, FORGET IT, I'M A SET IT, ON FIRE, LET IT BLAZE, FEEL THE FIRE, SO AMAZED TO THE CHOIR, I KNOW IT'S BEEN A WHILE, I KNOW YOU WALKED A MILE, BUT LET ME SEE YOU SMILE, EVEN WHEN THERE'S SADNESS I WALK THROUGH THE HAZARD, CHRIST PUT HIS HANDS AND HE RESURRECTED LAZARUS, UNIVERSAL THOUGHT, WHAT MATTER

IS THIS, WITHOUT GOD YOU DON'T EXIST, NOW SHOW ME WHERE THE EXIT.

IF YOUR HEART IS BUILT OF STONE, HOW WILL YOU EVER FIND YOUR WAY HOME, ONLY ONE MAN SITS ON THE THRONE, FORGET ABOUT ANY ERROR OR PAIN THAT MAY HAVE LEFT YOU IN VAIN, WASH AWAY THE SINS OF YOUR NAME, FOR HIS LOVE IS NOT THE SAME, HE WAS THE ONE WHO CAME, AND TOOK THE BLAME, AND LEFT THE FAME, ALL TO SEE YOU SMILE, I KNOW IT'S BEEN A WHILE, IT FEELS LIKE I WALKED FOREVER, WILL I EVER REACH HEAVEN, ONLY YOU, GOD'S SON, I KNOW MY NAME IS WRITTEN IN YOUR HEART, THIS LOVE BETWEEN YOU AND I, I DON'T EVEN NEED NO EYE, NOW I SEE WHY THE ANGELS CRY, YOU DIED FOR ME, IT TOOK

YOU TO A PLACE, YOU DIDN'T DOUBT ME, YOU ARE FOREVER KING, THE ANGELS FORVER SING.

I'M SECOND GUESSING, I'M JUST CONFESSING, I LEARNED A LESSON, LOVE IS GREATER WHEN YOU DEALING WITH THE FACTS, LOOK AT THE ROSE, IT GREW FROM THE CRACKS, CONCRETE, DON'T LISTEN TO THE DOUBTERS, OR THE UNBELIEVERS, IN THE STREET WHERE THEY WANT TO SEE US, CHRIST, GOD IN THE FLESH, I TELL HER WATCH HOW YOU DRESS, APPROACH LIFE WITH SINCERITY, NO COACH, THE GAME WHAT THEY SELLING ME, BUT I JUST LOOK TO THE MOST HIGH, CAUSE I KNOW I'M A FLY WHEN THERE'S NO SKY, OH WHY, DO I FEEL LIKE, HE PUT ME ON A PATH WHERE THERE'S NO LIGHT, HE KNOW I'M A SHINE REGARDLESS, I WAS BORN TO RISE, THEY JUST HEARTLESS, HUNGRY FOR

THE TRUTH THEY TRYING TO STARVE US, MY APPETITE FOR THE AFTER LIFE, AFTER THAT, WE JUST ACTING RIGHT, HOW SHOULD I SAY, ACTION... LIGHT.

MAYBE I AIN'T INSPIRED, MAYBE THE WORLD'S ON FIRE, WHY CAN'T WE TEACH OURSELVES TO REACH HIGHER, RUNNING FROM THE TRUTH, YOU A LIAR, NOT YOU BUT WHAT THIS SOCIETY STANDS FOR, IT'S

# 6 / 12

Like clapping and not knowing what your hands are for, war, against all odds, against all gods, only one will remain, the real name, Christ, his kingdom is higher than the breath of a cloud, his love brings to life the death of a cloud, he washes away pain, he touches the rain, his love didn't die even though he died, that's why the angels cried, but he rose, to resurrect the souls, he

RESTS ETERNALLY IN THOSE, LOOK DEEP, AND YOU'LL KNOW IT WAS YOU HE CHOSE, YOU ARE THAT ROSE.

I KNOW THIS PAIN HURTS, I KNOW THIS PEN WORKS, SO LET ME WRITE HOW I FEEL, THEY WON'T LET ME, CHRIST, THE EPITOME OF WHAT'S REAL, THEY WON'T GET RID OF ME, NO DEAL, NOTHING IN THIS WORLD WILL I ACCEPT, NOT EVEN EXCEPT, TO THE NIGHTS I HAVEN'T SLEPT, I KNEW THE MIRROR THEY DREW, BUT THE LORD HAS A CHOSEN FEW, WHAT DO I DO, NO OTHER CHOICE, NO OTHER VOICE, GOD IS SPEAKING, MY KNEES WEAKENED, THE HOLY SPIRIT IS THE CARRIER OF TRUTH, NO BARRIER OF PROOF, MY REFLECTION YEARNS FOR THE LOVE THAT MAKES MY SOUL CRY TEARS OF JOY, GIVE MY LORD MY HEART, NO DECOY, THIS

IS MORE THAN MUSIC WITH PASSION, THIS IS LANDING WITHOUT CRASHING, THEIR HEADS ABOVE THE CLOUDS, SILENCE IS NOT HEARD IN CROWDS, NO APPLAUSE, HIS HEART ON THE CROSS, HIS EYES LIGHT UP THE STARS, FORGIVE ME FATHER, THE WORLD IS NOT OURS.

THEY DON'T KNOW THE STRUGGLE, THE PAIN, THE LIGHT, AM I BLIND TO THE LIGHT, TELL ME WHERE WE HEADED, I DON'T KNOW IF WE THERE YET, CLEAR THE RUNWAY, BETTER YET CLEAR THE JET, NO PLANE, NO PAIN, HE DEALT WITH DEATH, HE FELT THE FLESH, HOW SHOULD I CONFESS, I CAN'T LEAVE, BUT MY HEART GOT TO BREATHE, CHRIST, I DON'T NEED ME, SO FAR, SO GONE, I DON'T KNOW I'M IF WRONG, BUT I KNOW I AIN'T RIGHT, I DON'T LIVE FOR THE HYPE, I DON'T LIVE FOR MY LIFE, I LIVE FOR THE

LORD, EVEN THROUGH THE WAR, I DON'T NEED NO AWARD, PRAISES TO THE MOST HIGH, NO POINT OF RETURN I'M SO FLY, DON'T LET THEM TELL YOU NO, TELL ME DO YOU KNOW.

THE PAIN AND THE MISERY, THE SAME WITH THE TENDENCY, I'M JUST TRYING TO FIGURE OUT, I'M JUST TRYING TO LIVE IT OUT, WE ABOUT, SEE NO DOUBT, LET US OUT, FREE MY PEOPLE, I SEE THE EVIL, I DON'T SEE NO EQUAL, THEY LIVING FOR THE LIFE, THEY TOOK A WRONG A TURN, YOU CAN'T GO AROUND FIRE AND NOT GET BURNED, DEAR MAMA I'M SORRY FOR THE PAIN I CAUSED, THE LORD DIED ON THE CROSS, FOR YOURS AND MINE, DO YOU MIND, TAKE A TIMEOUT. THIS YOU MUST FIND OUT.

THEY'VE BEEN PREPARING FOR WORLD WAR THREE SINCE I WAS THREE, NOW IT'S

ARMAGEDDON CAUSE I CAN SEE, THEIR LIES AND DECEIT HAVE NO USE FOR GOD, THE SEAT OF A FRAUD, WITH DEVILS I WON'T SIT, HIS BLOOD WAS INNOCENT, HEAVEN SENT, NO MAN KNOWS GOD ACCEPT FOR JESUS, YOU WONDER HOW HE COULD SEE US, WOULD HE BELIEVE US, WOULD HE RECEIVE US, BUT NO HE WILL NOT LEAVE US, THEY FAKE, THEY LOVE THEIR VISA'S AND MONA LISA'S.

# 7 / 12

My mind may have been defeated but my heart hasn't been deleted, my soul I need it, God will lead it, to the promise land, love's promise is to the nation who awaits Christ, as water turns to ice, as fire becomes their light, and the days become night, I'll look only to the Lord who brought me here, who caught fear and took it to the grave and rose the slave, He who saves, not hidden in caves.

HE EXPOSED THOSE WHO TOOK SOULS, CAUSE HE GAVE THE SPIRIT OF THE BROKEN, A BLAZE, NOT WHAT MAN SAYS, BLOCK THE SUNS RAYS, BUT THE LIGHT OF CHRIST MUST SHINE, LEAVE LUST BEHIND, AND MAKE THAT CLIMB, NO DIFFERENTIAL IN MY PRIME, ESSENTIAL IN MY TIME, NO ONE BUT THE MESSIAH, AS MY EYES ARE, I SAW, MARTIAL LAW, THE IMPARTIAL AWE.

DRIVEN WITH WHAT I'M GIVEN, LIFTING FOR WHAT I'M LIVING, SIT IN WHERE I FIT IN, HIDDEN, IN THE TEMPLE, SET THE EXAMPLE, WATCH THEM FLY AWAY, TO A BRIGHTER DAY, ALL I CAN SAY, GOD, THE MAKER, LIFE WITH NO MAKE UP, WE NEED TO WAKE UP, CHRIST DIED, HIS MOTHER CRIED, BUT HE ROSE LIKE A FLOWER, RAIN WHEN IT SHOWERS, NO MAN KNOWS THE HOUR, A LION CAN DEVOUR, BUT ONLY GOD HAS

THE POWER, THE WICKED HE WILL DESTROY, HIS PEOPLE HE WILL RESTORE, ASK GOD WILL WE SOAR.

THE TALENT YOU POSSESS CAUSES THE DEVIL STRESS, HE KNOWS YOU WERE BLESSED WITH GREAT HOPE, WITH PAIN HE CANNOT COPE, HE QUIT ON THE LORD, BUT DON'T YOU QUIT, CAUSE THAT'S WHEN THE DEVIL REAPS HAVOC, THIS WORLD YOU CAN HAVE IT, CHILDREN DYING, WHY HIM, CAUSE HIS HEART WAS WRITTEN WITH

ANGEL WINGS, ANGELS SING, THEY REFUSE TO LISTEN, THEY CHOOSE WHAT'S MISSING, LOST BUT NOW FOUND, THE CROWN, HE'LL BE HERE WHEN THE WORLD GOES DOWN, THEY SAY THEY RUN THE TOWN, I'M NOT EVEN FROM THIS PLANET, MY LIFE I COULDN'T HAVE PLANNED IT, LOVE IN MY HEART PLANTED, WALKING TILL I REACH FOREVER, BAPTIZED IN THE RIVER, THE LAST SURRENDER, LET US BOW OUR HEADS AND PRAY, CHRIST TAKE ME AWAY.

I REFUSE TO LOSE UNDER THESE CIRCUMSTANCES, MY HEART IS THE CANVAS, THESE WORDS PAINTED WITH EMOTION, THEY GOT THE WRONG NOTION, THINKING MY LIFE IS MIRRORED BY THEIR ACTIONS, I WON'T STOP AT SATISFACTION, I'M REACHING TILL THE WORLD IS NO LONGER AN ATTRACTION, BUT

JUST A DREAM DEFFERED, LIVING IN CHRIST IS PREFERRED THROUGH THE WORD OF GOD, YOU KNOW THEY PRETEND, THEY WILL NOT KNOW, WHEN HEAVEN SNOWS, IN THE RAIN I WAIT, FOR DAY I DON'T HATE, AND OPENED IS THE GATE, TIME IS NOT LATE, IS IT MY DESTINY OR IS IT FATE.

A MOMENT AFTER, NO LAUGHTER, TEARS OF A PASTOR, WHO CAN SAVE ME, WHO CAN ENSLAVE ME, MY THOUGHTS LOSE CONTROL, FEAR HAS TAKEN A HOLD, I RUN FROM THE PAST BUT WE MEET UP IN

# 8 / 12

THE STRANGEST MOMENTS, NO CHANGES CONDONE IT, LOST IN MEMORIES, HOPING THEY REMEMBER HOW I TRANSFORMED, I WAS BORN RISEN FROM THE STORM, PREDICATED I WOULD NOT BE THE NORM, CHOSEN, EXPOSING WHAT THEY CLOSING, ONE WORLD UNDER SATAN, HOW BLATANT OF A STATEMENT, UNDER GOD IS WHAT MAKES ME SO ODD, THEY CCOULDN'T LOOK IN HIS EYES CAUSE THEY KNEW HE'S THE ONLY ONE WHO COULD RISE, SURPRISE.

HE WAS SENT, THROUGH WHAT WASN'T MEANT, HIS LIFE HE TOOK DOWN TO REBUILD THE TEMPLE, HIS PRECIOUS BLOOD WAS THE ONLY EXAMPLE, IMMANUEL THE NAME OF THE LION THAT ROARED, TILL HE BECAME LORD, HIS PRESCENCE TO MANKIND ALTERED ANY PREVIOUS ATTEMPT TO LEAVE THE WORLD IN THE HAND OF A THIEF, WHO HAS LEFT THE WORLD WITH GRIEF, HIS RETURN, IN THE EYES OF DARKNESS IS CONCERN, FOR THEY HAVE NOT LEARNED, THEY LEAD THE BLIND BUT NEED THE BLIND, BUT THEY HAVE NOT SEEN ONLY IN THE MIND.

MAMA TOLD ME DON'T CATCH A CASE, PUT THE FLOWER IN A VASE, HARD HEADED NOT LISTENING TO WHAT THEY WERE TELLING ME, ALMOST CAUGHT IN WHAT THEY WERE SELLING

ME, NOT SELLING MY SOUL TO THE ENEMY, EVEN IF THEY PUT AN END TO ME, THEY WILL NOT ENTER ME, JUST GETTING STARTED, DEEPLY HEARTED IN MY JOURNEY TO REACH HEAVEN, PLEASE CALL THE REVEREND, THE MINISTER, MY THOUGHTS GETTING SINISTER, HELP ME LORD IN MY WILL TO HEAL, TO BE ONE WITH THE REAL, CAUSE I WON'T TAKE NO DEAL.

TAKE A LOOK, WE DON'T DO GOOD LUCK, SHARE MY THOUGHTS, TRAVEL THROUGH THEIR HEARTS, LIGHT FROM THE DARK, RIGHT FROM THE START, SITUATIONS AIN'T RIGHT, PICTURE WAITING FOR THE NIGHT, WE GETTING RICHER WITH THE LIGHT, WE FIGHTING FOR A TITLE, AIN'T NO WRITING FOR NO IDOL, WAS BORN TO BE THE ART, GOD THE PAINTER, GOT THE PAIN OF A SINNER, PRAYER FOR THE WINTER, PRAY

BEFORE YOU ENTER, UNTIL THE END OF TIME, CHRIST, THE ONLY END OF MIND.

MY THOUGHTS MOVE FASTER, MY THOUGHTS MOVE WITH LAUGHTER, MY THOUGHTS AIM FASTER, THE GAME AIN'T MASTERED, UNTIL YOU UNMASK HER, DEAR BEAUTY IS SOMETHING I CAN ASK HER, FILL MY GLASS UP, LIFE IS A MOVIE, PLEASE DON'T ACT UP, RACING TO THE FINISH LINE, DON'T BACK UP, ESCAPING THE PRISON CAUSE WE ALL LOCKED UP, EXCUSE ME I DON'T MEAN TO BE RUDE, SEEING GOD IN MY DREAMS, I DON'T SEE YOU, CHRIST THE REASON I SEE THRU, NOW I SEE YOU.

WE CONTINUE TO LIFT OUR HANDS, DAY BY DAY WE LIVE BY THE SAND, KNOWING ONE DAY THERE WILL BE NO MAN, OFF BREAD ALONE

MAN CANNOT STAND, STAND IN HIS PRESENCE, MAN WILL NOT RECITE HIS REFERENCE, HE WHO IS GOD PLEASE RISE UP, THAT DAY NOT EVEN THE SUN COULD RISE UP, WE WATCH THE RAIN, CAMERA SHOT, WATCH THE FLAME, AND IN THE END GOD MADE THE RIGHT CHOICE, AND IF YOU DON'T BELIEVE IN CHRIST THAT'S YOUR LAST CHOICE.

MY THOUGHTS IN THE CHURCH, THIS PAIN HURTS, HOPE IT DOESN'T GET WORSE, CAUSE IN THE END THERE'S NO PRETEND, I DON'T EVEN KNOW WHO'S MY TRUE FRIEND, SAY A PRAYER, I SEE YOU LATER, REACH ME AT THAT ELEVATOR, TELL ME WHY WITHOUT THE Z, I HOPE MY SON HE RESEMBLES ME, I HOPE THE LORD HE REMEMBERS ME, COLD NIGHTS, LONG FLIGHTS, HE DIED FOR ME, COMPLETE

INNOCENCE, IN THE SENSE CALL HIM JESUS, IN THE DARK HE CAN SEE US, WITH THE LIGHT HE CAN FREE US, WE TAKE IT TO A PLACE WHERE WE NEED LOVE, AIN'T NO OTHER OPTION BUT TO FREE YOUR HEART, CHRIST TOLD ME DON'T BE AFRAID OF THE DARK, YOUR SOUL AND I WILL NOT BE APART, I LOVE YOU MORE THAN YOUR HEART, MY LOVE FOR YOU IS ONLY THE START, WHERE DO I BEGIN, THIS LOVE WILL NOT END.

ARGUMENTS BY THE BEACH, I WAS TOLD THE STARS I COULDN'T REACH, MY SOUL IS THE ONLY WAY I TEACH, I MUST KISS THE LORD'S FEET, A HEAVENLY KISS IS HOW I GREET MOTHER EARTH, FORGIVE THE BIRTH, SO MANY PEOPLE BEEN HURT, YOU WERE TAKEN FROM THE DUST OF THE DIRT, REMAIN ALERT, STAY IN THE

PRISM OF ETERNITY, CHRIST IS THE IDEA OF ALL CENTURY, GOD IS ASKING WHEN WILL YOU RETURN TO ME.

I'M LIKE AN ASTEROID, ANYTIME I COULD CRASH, GOD TOLD ME DON'T WORRY ABOUT THE CASH, IN A MOMENT OF FLASH, I DECIDED, I WOULD WRITE IT, WASN'T INVITED, THE LORD WHO IS ETERNAL, MY THOUGHTS IN A JOURNAL, CHRIST, GOD'S SON, NOWHERE TO RUN, REPENT AND BELEIVE HE WAS SENT, TO RESCUE A GENERATION, BLESSED IN ALL NATIONS, THE DAY I HAVEN'T PRAYED, IT TOOK ME A COUPLE DAYS, TO REGAIN COMPOSURE, WE IN A WAR, I'M A SOLDIER, THE HOLY SPIRIT BRING ME CLOSER TO THE LORD, I KNOW I AIN'T PERFECT, HE DIED FOR ME WITH ALL HIS LOVE, ETERNAL LIFE, THAT'S LOVE, DON'T REJECT IT,

HE RESURRECTED, NOW HE'S HIGHLY ELECTED, SEATED AT THE THRONE, SEE WE ACT ALONE, BUT THEY TRACK MY PHONE, NO VOICEMAIL, YOU GOT TO SPEAK UP, THEY GOT THEY FEET UP, FREE US, NOW THEY CAN'T SEE US, IN THE NAME OF JESUS.

DON'T LET THE SPIRIT DIE, DON'T FORGET THE WIND CAN HEAR IT WHEN YOU CRY, A NEW SKY, LOVE IS BELIEVING YOU WERE MEANT TO BE WITH GOD, THEY CAN SEE YOU BUT DON'T WANT TO BE SEEN WITH YOU, WHEN WILL YOU ADMIT TO THE WORLD YOU LOVE CHRIST, THE BLIND DON'T NEED LIGHTS, THE DAYS DON'T NEED NIGHTS, ARE WE GOING TO LAND ON STARS, OR ARE WE STARS, WHAT IS YOUR HEART GOING TO SAY, WHAT IS YOUR HEART GOING TO PRAY, LET US SEE ANOTHER

DAY, I LOVE THE ONE WHO CARRIED MY SOUL FROM THE RIVERS OF DEATH AND LEFT ME WITH BREATH, AND THE SPIRIT IS THE ONLY THING LEFT, THESE WORDS ARE HEARD BY THE DEAF, TAKE ONE LAST BREATH.

# 10 / 12

I'M OFFICIAL, NO INITIAL, SO MANY ISSUES, DON'T KNOW WHAT'S THE FACT, MATTER OF FACT, I'M TAKING IT BACK, TO THE LORD I'M A DIE, AIN'T NO REASON WHY, I FELL BUT I ROSE AGAIN, I KNOW A FRIEND, I KNOW A MAN, NAMED JESUS, BELIEVE US, DESTRUCTION IS COMING, I AIN'T EVEN RUNNING, I'M A STAND TALL LIKE GOD WOULD, ON THE CROSS, WE CALL IT DIE WOOD, HOW COULD I MAINTAIN, I MUST FLY, AIRPLANE, GOD IS THE PILOT, BEAUTIFUL

AS VIOLET, NO VIOLENCE, NO SILENCE, THE VOICE YOU HEAR IS JUST THE LORD SPEAKING, THE VOICE YOU FEAR IS JUST YOUR HEART WEAKENED, THE SPIRIT AND THE SOUL, JUST MEETING, HOW LOVELY, RENDEZ VOUS, I LOVE YOU, FROM THE PAIN TO THE RAIN, I'M A STAND TILL WE MEET AGAIN, AFTER THAT THERE IS NO END, THE END.

DESTINY IS CALLING, NEXT TO ME THE SKY IS FALLING, I TURN TO GOD, I LEARN FROM GOD, WHEN YOU DIE FOR SOMEONE YOU LOVE, LOVE BECOMES EVERYTHING YOU LOVE, THEY CAN'T UNDERSTAND SO THEY PUT ME ON THE STAND, THEY SAY I LOST MY MIND, THEY SAY I LOST THE TIME, BUT I FOUND LOVE, HOW CAN I BE BLIND, PAY ATTENTION BEFORE THEY TAKE YOUR MIND, THAT'S WHAT MY HEART TOLD ME LAST NIGHT,

THAT'S WHY I GAVE JESUS MY HEART FOR THE FIRST TIME AND REALIZE WITHOUT HIM I WOULD OF LOST MY MIND.

WHAT DO YOU EQUATE, WHEN YOU CAN'T HATE, TOMORROW IS NOT A DATE, JUST A BROKEN PLATE, JUST TO CROSS MY FATE, ANYTHING THAT CANNOT LOVE, I CANNOT RELATE, TIME IS NOT LATE, JUST SOMETHING YOU CAN'T MAKE, THAT'S SOMETHING I COULDN'T TAKE, CAUSE LOVE IS NOT A MISTAKE, BEAUTY IS THE ONLY THING HUMANS CANNOT MAKE, CAUSE THAT WOULD BE THE EASIEST THING FOR THE DEVIL TO TAKE, WHEN I TALK TO GOD, THAT'S SOMETHING THE DEVIL CAN'T TAKE, AND I AIN'T EVEN GOT TO MEDITIATE, LET THEM HATE.

READY FOR WHAT AIN'T BEEN BEFORE, I AIN'T FOR WAR, FLY HIGH, I AIM FOR MORE, LET THE RAIN POOR, HEADED TO THE MAIN FLOOR, SEE GOD IN MY SIGHT, CHRIST IN MY LIGHT, CRIED SO MANY NIGHTS, YOU CAN FIND ME IN THE CITY WITH MANY LIGHTS, GAVE MY LIFE TO THE LORD, CAN'T SAVE MY LIFE IN THIS WAR, SEEN TOO MANY POOR, TOO MANY MORE, BEAUTIFUL AS THE SKY, A FUNERAL AS WE CRY, BUT THE LORD SAID LET THE DEAD BURY THE DEAD, AND DON'T ASK WHY, A LOT OF PAIN, A LOT OF RAIN, BUT WHEN WE DIE WE ALL GONNA BE THE SAME, I CAN'T LOSE MY TRUST, AND THAT'S THE STORY THEY DIDN'T TELL US.

IS LOVE THE MUSIC YOU HEAR, IS CHRIST THE BEAUTY THAT REMAINS NEAR, WE WALK WITH

ANGELS WHO PROTECT OUR SOUL, THE JOKERS OFFER MONEY, SEX AND GOLD, DON'T PUT GOD ON HOLD, FORGET EVERYTHING YOU'VE BEEN TOLD, JESUS IS THE MOST HIGH, HELL IS THE LOST SKY,

# 11 / 12

THE TRUTH DOESN'T NEED WHY, THE BEAUTY IS TO SEE ALL FLY, LOVE IS SOMETHING YOU CAN'T USE, YOU CAN ONLY BLESS IT AND WATCH IT LIGHT UP THE STARS, THIS WORLD IS NOT OURS.

IF LOVE WAS LOST, WOULD YOU LOOK FOR IT IN THE STARS, I'M FLYING, THIS WORLD AIN'T OURS, LOVE WITHOUT CAUSE, CAUSE IN THE END LIGHTNING STRIKES, WE MUST BEGIN TO LIGHT THE NIGHT, LIKE THE NIGHT WE AIN'T SCARED OF THE DARK, NEW CREATION IN THOUGHT,

NO MISTAKE MAN CAN ERASE, HIS STEPS NO MAN CAN RETRACE, CHRIST THE VISIONARY OF GOD'S FACE, WORDS WERE MEANT TO BE SAID, SO TELL ME WHAT GOD SAID, THEY TOLD ME GOD IS DEAD, I CRIED UNTIL MY EYES WERE RED, CAUSE THEY COULDN'T UNDERSTOOD WHAT WAS BEING SAID, HIS MERCY IS NOT DEAD, THESE ARE THE WORDS I SAID.

MY HEART AWAITS FOR THE GATES TO OPEN, MY DESTINY, MY FATE, I'M HOPING, LOOKING TO CHRIST TO SEE THE SUN RISE, THE ONE WHO LOVES IS SO WISE, THE BEAUTY IS IN GOD'S EYES, ILLUMINATI AND THEIR WICKED LIES, ONLY GOD PUTS FEAR IN MY EYES, HEAR THE CHILDREN CRY, YOU DON'T KNOW WHEN YOU WILL DIE, JUST LOOK TO THE SKY, AND LET YOUR SOUL FLY, PAIN COMES WITH THE

SPIRIT, RAIN IN YOUR HEART, ONLY GOD CAN HEAR IT, THE THUNDER, I DONT' FEAR IT, LOVE IS SPECIAL, ONLY MEANT FOR THE SOUL, WATCH THE EVIL UNFOLD, MONEY, HATE AND GOLD, A KING IS ONE WHO FEEDS THE POOR, THE END OF THE WORLD, WHAT DID YOU DIE FOR.

DAYS WHEN I TALKED TO THE NIGHT, I WAS TAUGHT TO WALK BY SIGHT, THAT'S WHY I NEARLY MISSED MY FLIGHT, YOU BETTER GET IT RIGHT, AND FOREVER WITNESS HIS LIGHT, IF YOU HAVEN'T SEEN TOMORROW THEN TODAY IS THE JUST THE FIRST, LOVE ME THROUGH MY WORST AND YOU WILL LOVE WITH NO CURSE, THE PAIN IS WHERE IT HURTS, GIVEN A CHANCE, THE FLOWER IS THE ONLY ONE WHO CAN DANCE, FELL ASLEEP IN GOD'S HANDS, MAY I ALWAYS KEEP GOD'S PLAN, AND FOREVER

FORGIVE ME IN THE MOTHERLAND, THERE'S A LESSON LEARNED IN EVERY MAN, THERE'S A BLESSING WHEREVER I STAND, CHRIST IS THE ONLY ASPECT OF LIFE MEN DON'T UNDERSTAND, ONCE YOU START FLYING YOU WILL NOT LAND, SHOULD I SAY AND.

I SAY MY LIFE COULDN'T GET ANY BETTER, TRAVEL THRU THE RAIN, JUST TO GET SOME WEATHER, WHETHER OR NOT, I'M A BE ALIVE OR NOT, I'M JUST TRYING TO FLY, BE AN ASTRONAUT, WHO IS GOD, SOMETHING THEY DON'T ASK A LOT, WE ALL NEED JESUS. THE EARTH NEEDS BELIEVERS, I'M IN CHURCH HOPING I CAN REACH MY HEART, HARDEST PART IS TRYING GET OUT OF THE DARK, REALLY I'M JUST TRYING TO GET OUT OF MY THOUGHTS, CAUGHT UP IN THE MIDST OF A DREAM, REALIZE WE AIN'T PLAYING

FOR THE SAME TEAM. THEY PLAGIARIZE, THIS THE AGE TO RISE, WE STILL LOST IN EDEN, THANK GOD I'M STILL BREATHING.

I DON'T CARE WHAT THEY OFFER, NO FEAR OF THE ROBBER, CAN'T SECOND GUESS, IN THE MOTHERLAND MY HEART IS BLESSED, ANGELIC HANDS CAUSE I NEED REST, CHRIST THE ATONEMENT OF OUR TRANSGRESSIONS, THE PRICE OF THE UNKNOWN CONFESSIONS, I KNOW HOW HARD LIFE HIT ME, BUT I KNOW GOD WITH ME, WITH FAITH YOU CAN CHANGE THE WORLD, WHEN YOU SAVED IT'S STRANGE HOW THEY MOVE THE WORLD, BUT I'M STILL WALKING THE HOLY ROAD, THE GOSPEL IS THE ONLY CODE.

Printed in the United States
by Baker & Taylor Publisher Services